CREATING YOUR POWER LIST

FIND YOUR ULTIMATE OCCUPATION

ROBERT L. TAYLOR, JR. CRPC®

BALBOA.PRESS

A DIVISION OF HAY HOUSE

Balboa Press books may be ordered through booksellers or by contacting:

Balboa Press
A Division of Hay House
1663 Liberty Drive
Bloomington, IN 47403
www.balboapress.com
844-682-1282

ISBN: 978-1-9822-5835-1 (sc)
ISBN: 978-1-9822-5836-8 (e)

Print information available on the last page.

Balboa Press rev. date: 11/27/2020

Dedication

This work is dedicated to my wife, Wendy, whose constant support, encouragement, and love has made so many things possible in my life.

Also, to my children, Courtney, Stephanie, Bobby, & Christopher who are a constant inspiration. To my Granddaughter, Emmie, who is always shining. 'I see the world in your eyes'...

And of course, to those that dared to attempt a different approach to discovering what they really desire in their lives. Your successes and feedback prompted this work that will hopefully help others meet with their own success.

Epigraph

"Ask yourself what makes you come alive and then go do that, because what the world needs is people who come alive".

Howard Thurman

Acknowledgment

Those clients mentioned by first name in this work, Richard, Rebecca, and Nancy, whose last names must remain anonymous in order to protect their privacy, thanks for your courage to dig deeper.

Introduction

If you are looking to make changes in your life, particularly in your line of work or occupation, then building yourself a **Power List** is a great and effective way to begin. I know because I have done it and so have several of my clients with whom I have shared this. Those who followed the steps in this workbook claim this process helped to move them to a better place. Isn't that where all of us want to be, in a better place?

This is a tool that you can begin to apply right away. I have designed this workbook in a way that allows you to apply the concepts as you read along. Just follow the steps as you go and see what unfolds. Like all tools, you will get out of it exactly what you put in. If it sits on your shelf, then you cannot expect to reap the rewards it may offer you. On the other hand, if you do a deep dive into the concepts and really work them, then I believe you can go anywhere. My hope is you find it within yourself to take that deep dive.

This workbook is only about 50 pages long with intention is to deliver the information to you in a manner so you can quickly get to work on creating your **Power List**. This work has gone through a few transformations before reaching what you now hold in your hand. It originally started as a series of webcasts intended to promote a website I had been working on. It then began to transform into a book before being born into this workbook. Where you start is not always where you end up.

If you really want to make a change in your working life, as I needed to do over 25 years ago, then getting to that place starts with asking yourself a very important question. It may be a vastly different question than what you have been asking yourself. If you think about it, you spend a great deal of your day asking yourself questions: What do I want to eat? What do I want to wear today? What movie or TV show do I want to watch? And on and on. Your day is full of questions. Some may be very simple questions and others more complex involving different levels of effort to get to the answers. All questions involve a need to gather some level of information before getting to the best answer. This morning when I asked myself what I wanted for breakfast; I opened the fridge to see what we had in stock to help me come to an answer. By doing a quick inventory I was able to decide that a cheese and mushroom omelet would work with what was currently available and would satisfy my hunger as well as provide the necessary fuel for my body. By comparison, if I asked myself what kind of car to get for my next vehicle then that question usually leads to several other questions that must be answered first before a decision can be made. You might contemplate the distance you drive on an annual basis, which would help to determine if you buy or lease. You might ask yourself the various uses that might be applied to the vehicle, which would separate a two-seat sports car from a van or utility vehicle. Cost and then financing are also considerations. The core process is not that different. It just involves more steps and is not beyond the mental capacity of most.

You get to the best answers by asking the right questions. The answers are typically already within your consciousness, but it takes the right questions to lure them out. Now that statement might alarm you, but, where else would the answer to what you really desire be hiding? Some components of the answer lie outside your consciousness, such as where to find the right opportunity or how to get to it. With the right question you know what to send your mind searching for both inside and outside. The answers are there and the process in this workbook will help you to dig them out. Like prospecting for gold, only the gold is not in the ground, it is inside you.

One morning not long ago as I lay in bed it dawned on me that this writing should include a note I wrote a few years ago to a group of my friends after spending a New Year's Eve with them. The title is called "Pandering for Mediocrity". There are those that are content with settling for whatever life tosses at them and working hard just to hang on. Then there are those that refuse to settle and are continually reaching for something better. There is a vast difference between these two types of people and their outcomes are the result of which thought process they decide to empower. Both sets of people can change their circumstances yet only one takes action to do so.

I like to share information I find useful and motivating, especially with those I care about. Often that information is of a probing nature and, therefore, uncomfortable – or downright offensive – to those who are not ready or willing to do the hard work it sometime takes to realize their ultimate self. However, I honestly believe what my wife's grandmother used to tell her all the time: "Nothing worthwhile is ever easy."

This is the letter I sent to my friends. I believe it gives a good framework to my belief in the fruitfulness of goal setting and the importance of perseverance.

Pandering For Mediocrity

So, here we are, January 2011, a new year, a time of rebirth if you will, a time to take on new perspective. A time for setting new goals, chart a new course, plan for bigger outcomes. This is a month when many of us look to the future with new hope and new expectations for a better year than the one we just came through.

Every year for the last 10 years I have taken the advice of motivational speaker Brian Tracy. I sit down and create a goal list for the upcoming year, fold it up and stuff it in an envelope then I put it in my top dresser drawer. This list usually includes about 10 items such as income objectives, some project objectives, health goals and so on. When I look back at these lists, I am very often surprised by the number of items that I have achieved. Some remain untouched or in the works but overall positive results for most. Mr. Tracy's point is that by committing these goal items to paper is a way of burning them into your sub-conscious thinking so that they have a better chance to take root and come to fruition. He is right! They do!

This past New Year's Eve we spent, what has become, our traditional New Years' Eve at one of our dear friends' home with the same group of friends that come together throughout the year for other celebrations. It is a lovely gathering with fine pickings and much laughter. It is usually a light evening with games, funny stories, and such. One past year I suggested that we all share with the group what our goals were for that following year. We made it around the table once with everyone's thought that was just that, 'the thought' for the moment. It was evident that no one had given much consideration to what they might attempt to accomplish or like to achieve in the coming year. This conversation quickly got me "voted off the island" for daring to suggest that we hold each other accountable to these goals throughout the coming year. I thought it might have been a good way for friends to support each other. I came to realize that these were not real goals that were spoken. They were more like whimsical or random thoughts. I began to fear that I was in the company of people I care about, love, and consider my friends but who were goal-less!!! How could this be? Anyway, I let it go, actually I had no choice I was voted off the island and therefore, my line of thinking was booted off with me.

This recent New Years' Eve I decided, and I don't know what prompted me to do so, to pose the question again! It seemed like enough time had passed and I was feeling like it was safe to come back onto the island. Perhaps it is my compulsion about the importance of setting goals for oneself. I journeyed down the road again, "What are your goals for 2011?" I asked those gathered. ...this time nothing...nothing! Not even a whimsical or random thought! One person actually said..."survive"! That word seemed to get a few nods around the table. The silence was deafening. It was all I could do to keep from falling out of my chair...and I was stone cold sober although I was well into 4 or 5 sparkling water's...

Just surviving, while very important, feels more to me like pandering for mediocrity. Of course, we all want to survive but how does just "surviving" have anything to do with our God-given right, no, God's **expectation** that we thrive? You may recall the Bible story of the Master that gave his 3 servants each some talents before he left on a journey. The first servant got 5 talents, the next servant 3 talents, and the last servant 1 talent. The gist of the story is that the Master expected that the talents he gave the servants would be put to good use. The first and second servant grew their talents substantially and were rewarded while the servant with only one talent was fearful of losing the one talent he was given and therefore did nothing to grow the given talent, not even earn interest on it. He just focused on protecting his one talent. The Master gave that servant's one talent to the servant with the most talents....

It strikes me that my friends are acting in the manner of the 3rd servant, out of fear of losing what they have. Will God be pleased with this approach? Will he reward them for protecting what they have by just planning on surviving? I fear not for my friends. I know it has been a very tough year and I also know that some have struggled for several years. Is it because they have been protecting vs. proactively growing and building? Is it because they spend more time thinking negative than having a positive attitude? Is the lack of having a real, proactive, positive goal for which to reach for that keeps them in survival mode? So many questions... I do not proclaim to know the answers to them it just feels to me that "just surviving" is not a pathway to any rewards.... especially none that God has in mind.

To look at the larger picture for a moment, if I may be so bold, what if this country took that view? What if all our leaders came out with an agenda that went something like this: For the next year, we are not going to focus at putting people back to work or reducing our national debt or pursue world peace… we are going to just plan on surviving! Good God where would we be? More importantly where would we end up? China would kick our butt…worse than they are now. Everyone would kick our butt because even the smallest, poorest country in the world has a goal. None of them seem to be saying, 'let's just plan on surviving'. Those countries that are the poorest have the good sense to at least ask for help or accept it when it is offered. And who do they ask for help? Is it someone that is just in survival mode? No, they turn to nations that are wealthier, proactive, and reaching higher.

Alright, so this note is a bit more than you bargained for on this cold January as we start this New Year…I'm sorry. My point is this. God has given us all 'talents', some more than others but nonetheless we have them. Put them to use. They are not meant to be put under a rock somewhere for safe keeping. Take what he has given you, for what he has given you is directly linked to where he wishes you to be. If you are not sure of where or what that is then spend time listening…he will tell you. Be thankful for them, but for the love of God put them to good use. Make your plan one of thriving not just surviving! If you do not know how then look around for someone who is and model yourself after them. You do not need to reinvent the wheel. "Success leaves clues", as Tony Robbins would say.

Here is my challenge to you. Make your own "Goal List" for 2011, if you do not already have one, and put it in your dresser drawer. Be realistic and be unrealistic. Think big. Reach for what you think is possible and impossible. Write it down. It is that simple yet that powerful! It is easy to say, oh… here goes Bob again, and fluff it off…prove me wrong. I dare you! Go ahead, prove to me that having a goal or two or three is not a worthy activity. Prove to me that making a list for yourself of things you want to achieve or pursue is a complete waste of your time. Prove to me that positive thinking does not pay a better dividend. You know what, forget about proving it to me…prove it to yourself!

Happy New Year

Bob

So, there you have it. I think this helps to give you a bit of understanding as to where my head was at when I developed the "Power List". So, if you are still with me after reading this forward then working on building your own "Power List" may be for you!

Foreword

While I did promise that we would get right to the main content and begin work, I believe it is important that I mention the current state our world is in and some additional thoughts. At this time most everything is shut down due to the Coronavirus or Covid-19 pandemic that has swept the globe. As a result, unemployment has gone from the lowest post World War II rate of about 3.6% to over 14% as of the end of March 2020 and in just a few short weeks. There are over 33 million people out of work at this moment and filing for unemployment, just in the United States. It is expected to get worse before it gets better. The U.S. government has expanded out unemployment compensation to 39 weeks and are paying some people more than they were earning in their normal jobs.

Many people have continued to work from home, even news anchors and reporters are broadcasting from their living rooms. Entertainers are putting on short performances from their home in an effort to raise money for the needy as well as to entertain those of us quarantined.

We are now going into our 3rd month of quarantine with only essential businesses, grocery and drug stores open and even those have dramatically changed their working models. Restaurants are either totally closed or only offering take out or delivery. Everyone is wearing masks and gloves to keep themselves and others safe. Our world has changed almost over-night.

During this time, I have been thinking a great deal about Nelson Mandela, who was the former President of South Africa from 1994 to 1999. Beginning in 1962, he spent 27 years in prison for political offenses and his efforts in trying to dismantle the country's apartheid system. When he was asked how he survived this time in prison or if he held great resentment against those that put him there, he would say he didn't waste time on those thoughts but, spent the time "preparing". I cannot help but think his actions and mental approach to surviving the situation is what helped elevate him to the office of President, which then helped to bring about real change to South Africa.

Someday we are all going to look back on this time of quarantine and ask ourselves or be asked by our children or grandchildren what we did while quarantined. I would like to be able to answer them in the same way as Nelson Mandela answered, "I prepared". While I expect my own job to remain mostly intact, there will certainly be some changes in how I do it and interact with people, but, for those who may have lost their job entirely or had been thinking of an occupation change anyway, could there be a better time to prepare and make those changes? This workbook and the concepts within can help you 'prepare' and rewire for what may be next.

Contents

1

Creating your Power List- Finding Your Ultimate Occupation

Hello, I'm Bob Taylor, a financial advisor with a large financial firm and the owner of a financial planning practice for the last 25+ years focused on helping individuals and families plan for their future financial goals such as retirement, education, areas of risk, tax strategies and estate planning.

Over these past 2 decades I have seen many folks struggling with sudden changes to their employment status and have witnessed their current and longer-term goals being disrupted. I have also engaged with those who have a burning desire to change from the position they currently hold. They were feeling burnt out or have just plain lost their desire to continue with the status quo. This presentation lays out a strategy that I have used many times to help those individuals chart their new course. Those of my clients who have chosen to fully engage themselves in this strategy have been able to move themselves past the place of discouragement, loss, and/or fear of the unknown to a better place where they not only are replacing their income, gaining security and control back, but more importantly, are finding more fulfillment in their life.

There is nothing much more difficult to handle than suddenly finding yourself misplaced and out of work. The company at which you have worked or have been employed for years was suddenly bought out or went out of business. Perhaps your job was eliminated, or you were terminated from your job. Whatever brought you to this place of transition was most likely unexpected. You may have thought that you would be at that job until the end of your workdays. Now what?

The job that you no longer have- regardless of how you felt about it or the company that gave it to you - was your security blanket, providing you and your family the means to survive financially. Its' loss has just rocked your world. It was what you depended upon to pay the bills, educate the kids, go on vacations, and save for the future. All that planning that you developed to address your many goals just went bust. It was perhaps the occupation in which you had a high level of expertise and knew so well that you could do the work in your sleep. Now it is gone! Is this sounding familiar?

When this type of thing happens, everything comes into question. How do you get through the next week or month? How do you keep up with the tuition costs for little Mary or Johnny? Yes, there are some unemployment benefits that will tide you over for the short term, but now you are faced with having to take money out of your IRA plan early or spend your 401k savings to meet the financial challenges immediately in front of you- not to mention the taxes and possible penalties it will cost you. It is a tough spot to be in for anyone.

The other issue I have seen is the person who hates their job, is just plain burnt out from it, or is bored and needs a change but doesn't know what to do to facilitate that change. You know that you really need to rewire but the plaguing question is: Rewire to what?

If any of this feels uncomfortably familiar, then keep reading. This strategy could change your life!

The dynamics that surround the almighty "paycheck" are significant. The fact that you are, or have been, working at a J-O-B instead of your dream occupation, career, opportunity, business venture, hobby or anything that could intensely stimulate you is most often at the core of this problem. You can blame the economy, the Congress, your many responsibilities, the dog or cat but at the end of the day you have to accept the fact that somewhere along the way you settled for a J-O-B and not YOUR dream occupation. This place where you have landed, as uncomfortable as it may be, presents you with an incredible opportunity to hit the reset button on your life and begin moving to a much better place. This is where "Building your Power List" comes in. This is not your typical to-do list, but a list that starts by asking yourself a very difficult question. Here is the **"key question": If you could wake up tomorrow and change your life by doing what you always dreamed of doing, what would it be?**

What is that one special passion that would get you out of bed early and moving? What is that special thing you just cannot wait to get to? Perhaps it is more than one thing. Perhaps there are many things. Maybe it is one or two things that you did earlier in your life and just never got back to. Could it be the item that is on your "someday" list? Is it possible that your answers to this Key Question will lead you to your next occupation? You might be very surprised at what it turns out to be.

The list I am suggesting you create encompasses the top 10 things you would love to go do starting tomorrow if YOU gave yourself the chance. This is YOUR list and it is HIGHLY personalized. It does not contain items that somebody else would like you to do. Do not even go there! Just you…your list…. It is all about you now, which may sound selfish, but there is a reason. It is about finding that new direction that will bring you true, long lasting happiness. And why shouldn't you be happy?

The place you are at right now, looking for a new direction, is a crossroad that cannot be taken lightly if you are to find -and live- your real passion in life. If you came home happy everyday instead of burnt out or depressed about your job, what would that do to your family life? Think about how a happier you will enrich your relationships with your spouse, children, family, friends and co-workers. Think about how less stress, more patience, and a higher level of self-confidence will positively affect your interactions with the people you care about, or how much better the important life decisions you make will be. Could a happier you lead to a much better place? You better believe it! The financial rewards will follow as well.

Now are you intrigued? Then let us get started on this mission.

To get started, get yourself a pencil then along with this workbook sit in a quiet place where you will not be disturbed and can focus.

STEP 1: When you are ready, in the space below write down the first 10 items that immediately come to mind to this *Key Question*: **If you could wake up tomorrow and change your life by doing what you always dreamed of doing, what would it be?**

1 _____

2 _____

3 _____

4 _____

5 _____

6 _____

7 _____

8 _____

9 _____

10 _____

Write the first things that come to your mind. You already have several things running around your brain that just need to be put down on paper. Get them on the list as fast as you can. This is called the Capture Phase.

The Capture Phase is interesting in that it can be very liberating. Just getting what may have been on your mind for a very long time written down is a way of empowering your goal and bringing you one step closer to giving it life. There is power in this action because you are not just writing your dream goal on a piece of paper and tucking it away somewhere like you may have done in the past. By writing your dreams and goals down you are tying them to the *Key Question* and acknowledging their importance to you. This is called **Attachment!**

Now back to building your Power List. It is important to try hard to get to 10 items on your list. Let your imagination run here and dig out those deep dreams, goals, and desires. For some of you, the last few items on your list may not show up so easily, but they are inside of you somewhere just waiting to come out. Try to keep yourself in a relaxed state and stay put until you get all 10 items written down.

I cannot stress enough how important identifying those items that you are most passionate about is to this process. The passion you may have for the goals you list provides the motivation you will need to attain those goals and dreams. Understandably, listing your deepest dreams and goals does not always come so easily. Many times, those dreams have been so covered over with the stress and discontent of your current life that they get lost and you must send out your emotional search party to find them again. I am certain you will find them by staying engaged in this process.

As I mentioned earlier, this is not your typical To-Do list. This is YOUR 'POWER LIST'. Its' intention is to be a Game Changer, a Life Changer, an Attitude Changer! If you can generate your Power List in 10 minutes that is fine, as long as this list of items has deep meaning to you then you have completed step one. If you need more time to get all 10 items in place, then take it. It is not about just coming up with 10 items so that you have a list. It is important that these items represent what you are passionate about.

No item is too silly or bizarre by the way.

The Power List starts with the action of dumping what is in your head, or heart, out onto paper. If you keep all your ideas, thoughts, and dreams in your head then they never have as great a chance to develop. They just keep spinning around. Get them down on paper and watch them begin to transform you. This is part of the power in creating your Power List.

STEP 2

Once you have 10 items on your Power List, prioritize it. Focus on what should be at the top, then second, and so on, until you have prioritized all 10 items. In the two columns below write your original list on the left then use the right column for the new order of priority.

POWER LIST:

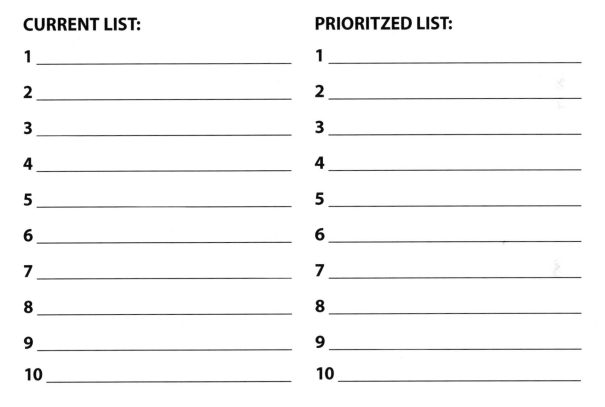

CURRENT LIST:

1 _____

2 _____

3 _____

4 _____

5 _____

6 _____

7 _____

8 _____

9 _____

10 _____

PRIORITZED LIST:

1 _____

2 _____

3 _____

4 _____

5 _____

6 _____

7 _____

8 _____

9 _____

10 _____

You might look at your list and discover that what you put down during your Capture Phase is already in your order of importance. You may discover, however, that what you uncovered in spaces 8, 9, or 10 should really be at the top. They could be the items that got buried and forgotten about. These items could end up being the most important on your list. Continue to contemplate your list and work the order until you feel good about the lineup. This could take a few days or a week.

2

Connecting the Dots

You are about to enter Part two of this series -**Connecting the Dots-Writing Your Power Statement**. I am sure that many of you had some illuminating moments during the creation of your Power List. Some of the clients with whom I have worked have said to me that when they looked at their list it did not even come close to what they had been doing for the past several years for employment. Some were working in jobs that had nothing to do with their true passions or goals. It just gave them a weekly paycheck. Now that you have your Power List, you can begin to look at things differently. Before we continue to the next step in this process, let's recap what we discussed in step one: It began by asking yourself the *Key Question*: **If you could wake up tomorrow and change your life by doing what you always dreamed of doing, what would it be?** You then began listing those items until you had a total of ten items on your Power list which represent your answer to this question. Then step 2 asked you to put the ten items in order of priority with the most important item in the number one position.

In this next section we are going to drill down deeper into your list and discover why these items made it onto your Power List.

Step 3

This step starts the same as the first, find a quiet place where you can focus on your Power List. Take the first item on your list and write that item next to the number one. In the lines that follow write a paragraph why this item is important to you. I call this your Power Statement. Let your emotions and passion about this item run wild. You are the only one looking at this list, so say what you really feel about this item. Is it a goal you have always dreamed of doing but never started, or a hobby you love doing and cannot get enough of? Use the most powerful language in your Power Statement that you can come up with to describe how you really feel about this first item on your Power List and how important it is to you that it comes to fruition.

For example, if your first item were to play guitar in a rock band and you simply wrote down: "Play guitar in a rock band because I really like music". How far do you think this statement is going to drive you? If you are like most people, it probably will not take you very far. But if you had a Power Statement something like: "Music has great meaning to me and is always playing in my car and home. I am always thinking about playing my guitar and it is never far from my thoughts. When I am playing the guitar, it is an expression of the passion and love I have for music and the instrument. When I am playing the guitar, it takes me to a different place where all my troubles melt away. When I am playing guitar in a band, I feel a connection that is beyond words and it is the most fulfilling activity that I do".

1 _____

_____

_____

_____

_____

2 _____

_____

_____

_____

_____

3 _____

_____

_____

_____

_____

4 _____

_____

_____

_____

_____

5 _____

_____

_____

_____

_____

6 _____

_____

_____

_____

_____

7 _____

_____

_____

_____

_____

8 _____

_____

_____

_____

_____

9 _____

_____

_____

_____

_____

10 _____

_____

_____

_____

_____

Once you feel your first item has a Power Statement attached to it, move on to the rest of the items, doing the same thing, until you have dug up from within you all the emotions you can find about each item on your Power List. Do not be humble! If you feel and have been told that you are an excellent guitar player, then tell yourself that; "I'm great at playing the guitar". No modesty for your Power List, just say it like it is.

It is important to identify how you feel about each item in a similar way. There is a tremendous effect on you psychologically over each item on your list when you take this approach. This will give you greater drive.

This exercise is just as important as when you captured the items on your list during the first steps. The intention is ATTACHMENT! Really dig out of yourself how you feel about these items and attach those feelings to the items on your Power List.

STEP 4

Now that you have created your Power List, organized them into order of priority, and have attached your Power Statement to each item, it is time to work on "Connecting the Dots".

This step works by looking at the items on your list to see if there is or can be a connection between them. For example, if your list contains items such as: social worker, accounting, stock broker, ministry, insurance representative, first responder, etc., you could easily break this down and pick one such as accounting, get training in the field and become an accountant. You could do that with any of the items on this list, but, when you are connecting the dots between items you are looking for something more: a way of combining one or more passions together in an effort to find an occupation that is far more fulfilling.

I am certainly not suggesting that this is easy to do. It may take a little work and research to find a common denominator, but it is certainly worth it in the end. This list, by the way, looked similar to mine. I enjoyed working with numbers, trading stocks, and a desire to help other people. Financial planners work in several of these areas and are generally people with the heart of a social worker and mind of a capitalist. It was a perfect fit for me and why I have been happy and successful in my career. I also took a first aid class and eventually became a first aid instructor. I worked and volunteered in that field for several years which was very fulfilling. As a first aider I have had to use those lifesaving skills many times and still do. The common ground between first aid instructor and financial advisor became evident from my Power List. Financial Advisor and First Aid Instructor combined several of the items from my list.

When you are trying to connect the dots on your list, you may want to consult with people that you may know in each of these areas to see what working in the field really looks like. You might talk with your accountant and ask him or her if they work with trading stocks, mutual funds, or insurance in their practice or are they just working with numbers on a computer all day. Whatever shape your list is beginning to take, part of your objective in this step is to think outside the box. Try thinking plural instead of singular. With the internet at our fingertips this task is not so cumbersome.

Real Life Examples:

One of my clients, Nancy, expressed how bored she was with her day and that her work was not giving her the entire fulfillment that she wanted or really needed. I asked her the **Key Question: If you could wake up tomorrow and change your life by doing what you always dreamed of doing, what would it be?** Her Power List did not exclude her work as a librarian, which she loved doing, instead, she discovered what she was missing that would help to complete her fulfillment. She missed working in the theater which she had done many years before having children and just never got back to. Her interest was not as an actress, but as part of the backstage production staff. As she completed the full process of building her Power List, she realized that she did not need to stop being a librarian but needed to get back involved with the theater. She discovered what was missing in her life, and not that she needed to totally rewire her life but to add to it. Her research uncovered that the local community theater group really needed help with their production staff, so she got involved and now spends a few nights a week going there after work. This discovery has changed the way she feels about her life.

Let me give you a couple of other real-life examples to help explain this step.

Becky, a client of mine, hated her job. She felt like it was draining the life blood out of her. She went through bouts of depression and chronic fatigue. This was not related directly to the job but going to a job that did not motivate or inspire her did not help. Additionally, Becky felt that she could contribute more to her family's finances by finding something that paid better, so she was motivated to consider her career options. When I asked her the **Key Question: If you could wake up tomorrow and change your life by doing what you always dreamed of doing, what would it be?** She began writing almost immediately. She had 3-4 items on her list before I could even finish explaining how the full process works.

These were her first four items:

1-help people to get healthier

2-give back to my community

3-stay healthy

4-find a more inspiring career

Part of Becky's story is that she had learned about some unique methods to address her medical conditions that the mainstream medical community did not even know about. Where their approaches did not help her, these other, less known, alternative methods did. She had incredible results from implementing them into her daily life. These methods allowed her to recapture her health and life. Any of you who have struggled with depression and/or chronic fatigue can well understand what Becky was going through. Because of her discovering how to apply those methods to her own life, she became compelled to share that information with others. She just did not realize how important to her doing that was until it showed up on her Power List in the number one spot. She also had not put that desire onto paper and looked at it in this manner, nor had she tried to connect the dots between this desire and her other items. Over the next few days, she completed her list of 10 items and emailed them back to me. As she began to work on prioritizing her list, adding her Power Statements, and then "Connecting the Dots", she began to see what was important to her could be related and applied to her search for her next, more inspiring, career.

The first discovery for Becky was a better understanding of just how important this first item was to her. More importantly, this discovery sparked a question in Becky's consciousness: Could this become one of the cornerstones for her to build her new career search on? By connecting item number one to items two and three, she began to see that there may be a way for her to combine these items and leverage them into a new career. Finding the common ground between her first three items could lead her to her fourth item: Finding a more inspiring career! Here is where this process has lead Becky:

She went on an Internet search and came up with a course of study that would give her a certification as a health coach! As she investigated what a health coach does, she realized this was the career for her. So, she spent a year taking a course that would make her a Certified Health Coach. Taking the course gave her the inspiration and drive she had been missing for many years. Becky achieved her certification and is now in the process of starting her health coaching business. Becoming a health coach is fulfilling her desire to help people get healthier. It is also a way of giving back to those in her community who may be going through similar health struggles and just do not know where to turn. She and her husband also sponsored a 5k run this past summer to benefit breast cancer patients – fulfilling item number two on her Power List.

While Becky is still in the early stages of her new career, I can tell you that her whole demeanor has changed. She loved taking the course of study and really feels that she has taken her life in a new and more inspiring direction. She also feels that she could do well financially and contribute more to her family needs. For Becky, creating her Power List led to a new and exciting chapter in her life allowing her to live her passion. It is important to note that not everyone's Power List will have such obvious connections between their items. If you do not immediately see a relationship between the items on your list, that is ok. Sometimes just having that one item on your list is enough for it to grab you and move you to action. This was the case in Richard's situation.

Richard had spent several decades working in a bank's mortgage department. He had been through several bank mergers which either displaced him or gave him a different employer. The last merger put him out of work at the age of 60. The first challenge for Richard was that he was at a difficult age to be hired by anyone. Employers tend to shy away from older hires due to elevated costs and expected duration of their employment. They sometimes look past the experience and knowledge base and focus only on the costs. The second challenge for Richard was that he was sick and tired of going through all of this "bank merger" business. He wanted to do something else that gave him more stability as well as more inspiration. Fortunately for Richard, his wife was still working, and he had some extended unemployment benefits to fall back on. So, there was a bit of time to sort it all out. Richard was not ready to retire and really wanted to accumulate more retirement assets. Ending his working life was not what he desired.

In our business meeting he shared all this unfortunate information with me. I then decided to ask him the *Key Question*: **If you could wake up tomorrow and change your life by doing what you always dreamed of doing, what would it be?**

Richard listened to me explain the strategy but did not start writing right away as Becky had done. He needed to spend some time contemplating the question first. About a week later I received his Power List by email. Here is what it looked like:

1-Accountant

2-Own a car dealership

3-Operations manager-community bank

4-Property manager

5-Writer-novelist

6-Writer-advertising

7-Office manager-medical; auto dealership

8-On-line music station

9-Management reporting

10-Actor

As you can see, he had a diverse set of interests. He also included a note that he would work on prioritizing the items and get back to me. It seemed clear that he was taking this strategy seriously. Well, time went by, and I had not heard from him in almost a year. I called to suggest we get together and review his financial plan and accounts. I also asked what he had been doing. In the back of my mind I presumed that he dropped the Power List strategy and moved on to something else. To my astonishment he responded: "I just finished writing my first book"! Item number five on his Power List. I was amazed! I was even more amazed when he shared the first draft with me. I could not put the book down! It was a murder mystery within, none other than, the banking business in our town! I truly enjoyed reading it and was surprised by his talent.

While he was writing his book, he kept searching for a new and different working position. Shortly after finishing his book, he landed a position as an assistant delinquent tax collector in an area city and really enjoyed the work. Since then he has gone on to take charge of the delinquent tax collection department of another, larger city for even more money. This position has aligned with several of the items on his Power List -- accountant, office management and reporting, as well as property manager.

Recently I asked Richard how he felt creating his Power List had helped him. He said that it really helped him to realize just how important it was to him to begin writing. Seeing "writer" on his Power List and then spending time organizing and prioritizing his list really brought that desire into focus. He also told me he is working on his 2nd book, which I cannot wait to read. Similar to the earlier story with Nancy, Richard was not making an extreme, bold, and risky career change to become only a writer. He was adding to his life the desire to write. He was able to connect other items together on his list which led him to a new inspiring occupation and generated immediate income. More income than he ever earned! This allowed him, along with his wife's income, to support his writing efforts as well as to continue to save towards their retirement goals. Eventually his writing could bring in a significant income, but he understands the importance of first allowing his writing skills to develop over time.

So, while I have suggested to you to let your thoughts and emotions run wild when developing your Power List, keep in mind you are creating a Power List to help lead you to your next occupation. You must think clearly through this and separate out what can be a fulfilling occupation and what is just a fulfilling hobby or activity. This is not to say that your hobbies cannot be transformed into something more significant, but sometimes the two do not work together. I love to cook and find it very medicinal at times. Transforming what I love to do in my own kitchen and for my own family into what it takes to operate in a professional restaurant kitchen daily tends to lose its' appeal very quickly. However, taking a cooking class to broaden my knowledge of cooking might be exciting and add a new dimension to my home cooking experience. I have a kitchen in my office, so occasionally I find pleasure in cooking up something for my partners and staff. In this small way I share something I am passionate about and that gives me pleasure. Alternately, my wife and I are also musicians and song writers. We have performed together many times over the years, which has generated income as a part-time occupation. By contrast we have also written, recorded, and released an album which was very fulfilling, but not yet an income generating occupation. Someday it may be more, but it is still a very fulfilling activity. The point here is we have not loaded up the van and hit the road into the unknown. We have our musical lives in the necessary place and not disruptive to our financial requirements. It is important to examine the needs and desires in your current life situation and then align your list, and the opportunities you see in that list, with those needs.

To recap this section, we started with your completed and prioritized Power List which are the ten items most important to you and in the order of their importance. Then we talked about attaching the emotional aspect, your Power Statement, to each item by adding a powerful emotional explanation of why each goal was important enough to find its' way onto your Power List. We then discussed the importance of attempting to find any common ground between each item by Connecting the Dots, and I gave you several examples of how myself and others have managed to do this.

There is a very important third step to the Power List strategy that I will share with you in the next and final chapter: Implementation! I will be discussing how to put your Power List into motion by building a Plan of Action. I believe this to be the most important step. You can create all the Power Lists that you want and attach all the Power Statements you can muster to it, but, unless you have an effective, actionable plan that you implement then you have just wasted your time and energy.

The two steps we discussed in this chapter are your next important steps in this process. Be aware that these steps are critical and must be done before continuing onto the last step:

"Putting Your Power List into Motion" where I will show you how to create your Action Plan.

3

Putting Your Power List into Motion

Motion- def.-the action or process of moving or being moved.

They say you cannot hit a moving target. If you are not in motion, then what can hit you is procrastination and depression, or many other things that can keep you from your goals. If you have reached this third chapter, you have completed your assignments by giving great thought to where you wish to go, congratulations! You are proving to yourself that you are serious about achieving your goal or goals and they are important to you. Take some time to celebrate!

What you do next will determine your outcome. It is the amount and size of your action that will determine the success of your outcome. By creating your **Power List,** you can now begin moving yourself to a better situation that is more fitting to what you are most passionate about! Let's get into MOTION.

Let us first recap the steps that I previously addressed in the first two chapters. It began by asking yourself this very important *Key Question:* **If you could wake up tomorrow and change your life by doing what you always dreamed of doing, what would it be?** You then captured the top ten items that answered this question and listed them. I asked you to list these items in order of their importance to you. In Chapter two I outlined the next step

ROBERT L. TAYLOR, JR. CRPC®

in this process, **Power Statements**, which involved attaching to each of the ten items on your Power List specific and passionate reasons as to why each item is important to you. Once you completed those steps, I asked that you try to see what common ground might exist between each item. So far, I have asked you to do what was most likely a lot of work but, look at what you have accomplished: You have composed your **Power List**! What is it telling you? How does it make you feel? Staring back at you from this Power List are strong desires and creative ideas that you have been carrying around inside you for quite a while. This list is telling you a story about yourself! It is finally out, and it is not to be taken lightly! Congratulations! With such a compelling list of opportunities in front of you, the only question you need to ask yourself now is: When do I start? When do I get into Motion?

How often have we all made plans to do something but, for whatever reason, never started on it? Maybe it is finishing or repainting a room in your house. Perhaps it is planning a trip or searching for an old friend who you may have lost contact with over the years. Have those plans just ended up in the 'someday' pile with all your other dreams and desires? I know for a long time that was how it went with me. I would start out in a direction on a project, be all inspired and excited, yet somehow, never see the finish line. Something would easily find its way between me and that finish line because I didn't have a Plan of Action (POA) laid out from the start that was effective enough to keep me on track and in motion so I allowed distractions to derail me. When I learned about this strategy of identifying goals, attaching the emotional components to them, and then building a Plan of Action (POA) to begin working towards those goals, it all started to come together. Of course, like most of us, I would try to take a short cut occasionally. I soon learned that if I skipped one of the steps then things eventually fell apart. I do not want to see that happen to you. So, please take note, this last step needs to be taken seriously. This Plan of Action, POA, will become the launching pad for your Power List, and it will lead you to where you really want to go! However, IT IS IMPORTANT that you follow your own well-defined POA and stay in motion. If along the way you feel it is not getting you to where you wish to go, then modify it.

Before you start building your POA, let me suggest that you keep this thought very much in mind: When building your **Get-in-Motion Steps** try to limit the steps to no more than four or five, it will be less overwhelming. If you build 10-12 steps for an activity it may be more distracting than useful.

So, you now have your prioritized Power List in front of you. You have attached the emotional component to each item and have connected the dots between those that can be connected. Using the following layout, let's start your POA with the first item on your Power List since it is the most important to you.

PLAN OF ACTION

You might want to make copies of this page for additional goals.

GOAL_____

DESIRED RESULTS:_____.

GET IN MOTION STEPS:

STEP
1_____

STEP
2_____

STEP
3_____

STEP
4_____

STEP
5_____

4

Final Points

POINT 1-

I believe it is important to Build yourself a ***Success Motivator***. Everyone needs encouragement and meeting with success is the best encouragement. When you are successful at something, no matter how big or small that something may be, it will motivate you. Your juices begin to flow, and you get inspired, which ignites the encouragement to keep moving forward.

I see this all the time in my 20-year-old Son who is quite the baseball player. Of course, his early efforts at simply catching or hitting the ball started like most kids, a bit rough. His love for the game and desire to be a great ball player drove him and kept him working at building his skills. Early on, the small successes he experienced gave him encouragement. Just starting to catch the ball that I tossed to him at the age of 9, as small a success as it was, we celebrated in a bigger way and this eventually became his ***Success Motivator*** and drove him to work harder. Along the way we did the same, made a big deal out of a great catch in the outfield or throwing a runner out at the plate or big hit. All these actions lifted his spirits, gave him confidence and inspired him to keep working harder because he was seeing great results. Over the years, when he did not get the results he was looking for, he then realized he needed to either dig down deeper, work harder, or rework his Plan of Action. What he learned was the desired results were really driven by the **Success Motivator** he built internally for himself.

Just getting a project started is often the hardest part. I believe if we focus on all that is involved to get to the finish line of most any project it stops us from ever getting started in the first place. Once you have your goal or goals listed out as well as what is required to get to those goals, I suggest you break your actions down into smaller bits that are easier to wrap your head around. Completion of each of these small bits can then become your **Success Motivator** and with each **Success Motivator** you experience it helps to propel you to the next step in the project and this is how you can move yourself through your project. And don't forget to celebrate these small successes too!

Let me give you an example:

Recently my wife and I decided to add a bathroom to one area of our home. I also decided to attempt the work on my own, at least the parts I felt I could handle. Being the planner that I am, I first sat down and worked up a set of drawings based on our desired outcome. This included taking measurements, a parts list, shopping online for cabinets and fixtures, and discussions...lots of discussions.

I then began to lay out the steps needed to get to our outcome. At one point I stepped back and looked at all that was involved in this project and I started to feel overwhelmed. I thought about the amount of work and time it would take to get this bathroom completed and I began to have doubts. I was fretting! That could have stopped the project right there from ever getting started. In the past it may have. All my actions were spent on what I wanted, the planning phase, and not on the action phase, all because I allowed myself to be overwhelmed by the amount of work involved. It created disabling self-doubt. This is where things can easily get derailed.

But here I was with our goal laid out and all the plans I needed to achieve this goal, I was not about to disappoint my wife, so I decided to break this big project into smaller and more manageable bits. This project needed to begin with some demolition. Well I can take anything apart, it is putting it back together that is challenging, so this bit should be easy. I got into motion taking things apart. When I finished the demo part, I did get a small sense of accomplishment. This became a **Success Motivator,** granted it was a small motivator, but nonetheless a motivator, so I moved on to the next small step: Framing. You should know this project is ongoing as I write this text, so I'll have to follow up with you on how it turns out, however, just yesterday I did some framing and I can tell you today I feel more motivated. It went according to plan, so my confidence level is elevated. I can honestly say I cannot wait to get back to work and onto the next step. This step has become another **Success Motivator**.

Build yourself a Success Motivator.

POINT 2

Consider getting yourself a Coach. Someone who will take a vested interest in helping you get started and stay on task. You may only need to have a coach for one or two items and not the whole list, but a great coach can make the difference between action and inaction, success and failure. You can consider a formal arrangement with a professional coach or just someone you know who has the knack for being a great cheerleader and can help lift your spirits while keeping you accountable to yourself. I have hired a few different coaches in my life and have had awesome results by just telling them what I want to accomplish then sharing with them issues that had become obstacles along the way. Someone who acts as your "sounding board" can be very beneficial as well. So often I see people getting tangled up in the minutia and losing their way towards their objective. A good coach will identify that behavior and help to get you back on track.

POINT 3

This point and arguably the most important is Attitude. Attitude is everything! Ask yourself how your attitude is. Ask those around you what they think of your attitude. Ask them to be truthful with you. Be truthful with yourself. If you are going through a rough patch in your life and you keep dwelling on the difficulties you are experiencing then certainly you might feel justified in having negative feelings and a compromised attitude. I get that.

Here is my advice: GET OVER IT! MOVE ON! STOP THE PITY PARTY!

It is holding you back! If you just can't seem to put it behind you then you may need professional counseling...then get it!

Now that you have gone through the process of building your Power List, ask yourself what type of attitude you think is going to be the healthiest and most helpful as you implement your Power List and head in a new direction -- a positive attitude or a negative attitude?

Bad attitudes sink ships! It's that simple. A negative attitude is not going to reap you the rewards you seek. Negativity just sucks the oxygen right out of the room. A positive attitude pays a better dividend.

There is lots of information out there on how to live a more positive life. If you are struggling with an attitude issue, I suggest you seek out help. A book I read a long time back by Lynn Grabhorn, "Excuse Me Your Life Is Waiting", is one such resource. She talks about how she turned her business completely around by changing her attitude, ending the pity party, and starting to think and speak only in positive ways. She had a powerful turnaround.

As for myself, I try very hard to stay away from people with bad or negative attitudes. I have dropped clients with negative attitudes, eliminated acquaintances with negative attitudes, and try to align myself with only goal oriented, positive thinking and speaking folks. It is sometimes difficult, especially if it is family, but it is certainly worth it in the end.

It is important that you realize you are on the cusp of taking action, if you haven't already, towards dreams and goals on *your* Power List which mean a great, great deal to you. Please do not allow a negative or bad attitude keep you from realizing a more fulfilling and inspiring future for yourself and those you love. Take the steps necessary to work your frame of mind into a more positive, productive state. A great, positive attitude is a very powerful force.

POINT 4

The final point I'd like to share with you is **Visualization**. This can be a game changer in many ways. Visualizing yourself fully engaged, successful, and achieving every item on your Power List is powerful. Think about professional athletes for a moment. Most pro golfers, for example, will walk onto the hitting tee, place their ball on the ground, then step back and look at their ball and where they want it to go. They visualize their back swing coming back away from the ball, then through and hitting the ball, the ball leaving the tee, the flight of the ball, and landing exactly where they want it to be. Then they walk up to the ball and act on that visualization. Pro baseball players will do the same thing before stepping into the batter's box. They spend a few moments while on deck picturing the ball leaving the pitcher's hand, traveling towards the plate, a perfect swing of the bat, the ball leaving the bat, and going to a certain spot on the field. Visualization is very powerful. It trains the mind to focus on your outcome then the rest of you just needs to follow along. In one of my previous examples I spoke about Becky. Through the process of building her Power List she was able to identify an occupation that aligned with her deep interest and passion of becoming a Health Coach. In her case, utilizing a visualization strategy might involve sitting in a quiet place, picturing a client in front of her while listening closely to the client tell their story. Perhaps she would then see herself giving great advice to the client and picture the client happily taking it, then implementing the strategies, and witnessing the client succeed with the implementation. She might then picture her practice growing and growing while feeling a strong sense of satisfaction. Visualization takes some practice, but the more you use it, the more you find how powerful it can be. It is one of my favorite strategies to use to attain a goal.

I have a picture in my mind, a visualization of this bathroom project and how it will look in the end, how I will feel accomplishing the project, and how convenient it will be to have a bathroom in that part of our home.

My hope is that this strategy of building your Power List helps to lead you to your next awesome occupation and implement real change in your life. It all starts by changing the questions that you ask yourself by asking the **Key Question: If you could wake up tomorrow and change your life by doing what you always dreamed of doing, what would it be?**

The power of having your biggest dreams and desires laid out in an order of priority is alone empowering, but, when you begin adding your Power Statement to each of these items you begin to realize their importance to you. Once you have completed these steps then bringing your Power List to life happens through the implementation of a well-designed Plan of Action and a Success Motivator.

Best of luck.

Printed in the United States
By Bookmasters